'*Towards a National Spirit*':
Collecting and Publishing in the
Early Republic to 1830

'Towards a National Spirit': Collecting and Publishing in the Early Republic to 1830

by WHITFIELD J. BELL, JR.

Delivered on the occasion of the

sixth annual Bromsen Lecture

April 29, 1978

BOSTON

Trustees of the Public Library of the City of Boston

1979

Maury A. Bromsen Lecture
in Humanistic Bibliography, No. 6

Library of Congress Cataloging in Publication Data
Bell, Whitfield Jenks, Jr.
 'Towards a national spirit'.
 (Maury A. Bromsen lecture in humanistic bibliography; no. 6)
 1. United States—Historiography—Addresses, essays,
lectures. 2. United States—History—Societies, etc.—
Addresses, essays, lectures. I. Title. II. Series.
E175.1.B44   973′.07′2   78-10486
ISBN 0-89073-057-1

Foreword

The Boston Public Library is pleased to present in book form the sixth Maury A. Bromsen Lecture in Humanistic Bibliography.

As Boston and Massachusetts approach their 350th anniversary in 1980, it is most appropriate that we look back to the early days of the Republic and assess the country's collecting and publishing activities. Dr. Whitfield J. Bell, the Executive Officer and Librarian of the American Philosophical Society in Philadelphia, the oldest learned society in the United States, was introduced by Stephen A. Riley, a member of the Bromsen Advisory Committee and the Director Emeritus of the Massachusetts Historical Society.

Dr. Bell, a graduate of Dickinson College, did his graduate work at the University of Pennsylvania. He taught history at his *alma mater*, where he served as Boyd Lee Spahr Professor before joining the Benjamin Franklin project in 1954 first as Assistant and then Associate Editor of the *Papers of Benjamin Franklin*. In 1961 Dr. Bell was appointed Associate Librarian of the American Philosophical Society and five years later he was appointed Librarian. As Librarian, prolific author and editor, and as advisor to many historical societies and commissions, Dr. Bell has made significant contributions to American research scholarship and we are pleased to add the 1978 Bromsen Lecture to this list.

PHILIP J. McNIFF
DIRECTOR AND LIBRARIAN

Introduction

Our speaker this evening is Whitfield J. Bell, the Executive Officer and Librarian of the American Philosophical Society in Philadelphia, the oldest learned society in this country. Founded in 1743, it is now world famous for its outstanding collections on "science since 1700, Benjamin Franklin and his circle, Darwin, evolution and genetics, quantum physics, and American Indian linguistics." Its aim continues to be the promotion of useful knowledge by collecting, preserving and publishing its scholarly materials. Those familiar with its printed *Transactions* will admit happily that the Society has succeeded admirably in its role.

It might as well be confessed here that Boston-born Benjamin Franklin was the founder. Indeed, there were those earlier Bostonians who felt that the American Philosophical Society might never have come into existence had not Franklin been exported to Philadelphia for that express purpose. Oliver Wendell Holmes, the Autocrat, Mr. Bell informs me, excused Franklin's aberration by saying that "he dwelt a while in Philadelphia." "Not so," countered Weir Mitchell, the writer, "Franklin was born in Philadelphia at the age of 17."

vii

Perhaps to avoid such a complication in the future, Mr. Bell chose to be born in Newburgh, New York. He assumed a degree of protective coloration, however, by attending Dickinson College in Carlisle, Pa., and by doing his doctoral work at the University of Pennsylvania in Philadelphia. With his formal training behind him, Mr. Bell embarked on a career that found him progressively the Boyd Lee Spahr Professor of American History at Dickinson College, the Visiting Editor of the *William and Mary Quarterly*, first Assistant, then Associate, Editor of *The Papers of Benjamin Franklin*, jointly sponsored by the American Philosophical Society and Yale University, and finally his present position for which he seemed preordained.

Preordained, for Whit Bell's chief interests have long been those of the American Philosophical Society: namely, Benjamin Franklin, early American science and medicine, learned societies, and bookshops. Whether vacationing on Cape Cod, or visiting in Boston, Washington, or wherever, Whit Bell quickly locates the bookshops. He is not only an avid collector of books and manuscripts, but also a true scholar who delights in sharing his findings with others. How else can we account for his publication record: 13 books, either written or edited by him, and about 150 articles, etc., on a wide variety of subjects. I was delighted to find listed, in addition to his numerous bibliographical articles, such intriguing titles as: "The Mother of Franklin's Son Again," "[Sherlock] Holmes and History," printed in the *Baker Street Journal*, and "Everett T. Tomlinson, New Jersey Novelist of the American Revolution." Perhaps many of you will remember with nostalgia Mr. Tomlinson's boys' books. Lyman H. Butterfield, the distinguished Editor-in-Chief Emeritus of the Adams Papers, best expressed the charm of Mr. Bell's writing. In a foreword to Bell's *Early American Science: Needs and Opportunities for Study* (Williamsburg, Institute of Early American History, 1955),

viii

Mr. Butterfield wrote: "Mr. Bell . . . was invited to prepare the present survey not only because he is an experienced scholar and bibliographer in the field but because he writes spiritedly even when listing works by and about a scientific author."

There is no doubt about Mr. Bell's established reputation as a bibliographer and humanist. That he follows a way of life centered on human interests I can vouch for. One need only accompany him on a visit to the famous Philadelphia open market to see his eye brighten and his step become even more purposeful. There I was introduced to shoo-fly pie and my wife, later, to real Philadelphia scrapple. If you are truly lucky, you may one spring evening after a fine dinner be given a tour of historic Philadelphia by Whit Bell, a tour that you will long remember.

STEPHEN T. RILEY

'Towards a National Spirit': Collecting and Publishing in the Early Republic to 1830

THE CREATION OF AMERICA was not the work of a day, nor yet a matter of constitutions and treaties, railroads, factories, and trade balances. America became a nation only slowly, many strands binding the fabric. As long as 35 years after the close of the War for Independence, in 1816, Peter S. Du Ponceau, Philadelphia lawyer and scholar, could tell his aged friend Charles Thomson, who had been secretary of the Continental Congress, that "a National Spirit . . . [is] yet to be created." From the Treaty of Paris until long after the Treaty of Ghent others were no less concerned than Du Ponceau that "a national spirit" be formed; and among those who, like him, fashioned it, in addition to farsighted statesmen, victorious generals, and the people themselves at their daily work, were poets and preachers and historians.

Unlike Britain, France, and other ancient states of Europe, America arose entirely in the age of writing, printing, and publishing. There was hardly an event in American history, from Columbus' discovery to the latest land survey in Indiana, that had not left a record of itself on paper, stone, or the land itself. No other country's origins were so fully documented, so easily recoverable and identified. "Among the singular advantages which are enjoyed by the people of these UNITED STATES," the Massachusetts Historical Society declared in its "Introductory Address" in 1791,

> none is more conspicuous than the facility of tracing the origin and progress of our several plantations. Derived from nations in which the means of literary improvement were familiar, we are able to ascertain with precision many circumstances, the knowledge of which must have been either disfigured or lost among a people rude and unlettered.

History here seemed to fill an especially critical function as a link that united all Americans. Of various nationalities and religions, differing in their experiences in both Europe and the New World, separated by wide distances, moving in and out of jobs and classes (one Philadelphian described himself successively—and correctly—between 1730 and 1765 as carpenter, builder, and gentleman), the Americans were bound to one another partly by their common history and its attendant myths. History, asserted Benjamin Trumbull, minister of North Haven and author of a *Complete History of Connecticut, Civil and Ecclesiastical* (1797) and of a *General History of the United States* (1810), would bring the citizens of America "into a more general acquaintance with each other, awaken their mutual sympathies, promote their union and general welfare." The nationalizing role of history at the end of the 18th century was hardly less important than in the 20th, when Steuben, Kosciusko, and Haym Salomon have been employed to link newer Americans with the older tradition.

In the decade between the Stamp Act and the outbreak of war ten years later sentiments of American national self-consciousness were clearly expressed. Reacting to British policies, for example, Americans through societies of arts strove to make their agriculture more productive, establish domestic manufactures, and improve the channels of navigation and trade. Americans travelling abroad, to take another, more intimate example, were regarded not as Virginians or New Yorkers, but as Americans; they accepted the description, then claimed it proudly, as one may see on the matriculation rolls of Edinburgh University, where, after 1760, here and there a medical student identified himself not "Pensilvaniensis" or "Virginiensis," but "Americanus."

It was to be expected that historians should be at work in the American colonies by mid-century. After all, more than 100 years had passed since the first settlements were made. The men of 1765 were as distant in time from Jamestown and Plymouth as we are from John Quincy Adams and the election of Andrew Jackson; curiosity about the past would alone have stimulated inquiry. During the first half of the century, for example, histories of Virginia were composed by Robert Beverley (1705) and William Stith (1747), and the Scottish-born Boston physician William Douglass wrote *A Summary, Historical and Political, of the First Planting . . . and Present State of the British Settlements in North America* (1755). In Boston too the Reverend Mr. Thomas Prince made a collection of historical materials and published one volume of a history of New England (1736) before turning away to other things. After mid-century the controversies between the colonies and Britain and between colonies with disputed boundaries provided additional incentive to historical inquiry and writing: history might throw light on the origins of the disputes and provide factual data for legal claims. Much of the constitutional debate of 1754–75 cited history, and was persuasive in some measure precisely because it rested so firmly on an understanding of human character and conduct. To this period we owe William Smith's history of New York (1757), Samuel Smith's of New Jersey (1765), and Thomas Hutchinson's of Massachusetts (1764).

The successful conclusion of the Revolution gave a remarkable stimulus to historical inquiry. It was widely recognized that that event was in many respects unique in the history of the world; and Americans cheerfully accepted the obligation they felt they owed themselves, Europe, and posterity to record and explain what had actually happened. "The new histories of America, which are already, in some measure, promised to the public," declared the *Pennsylvania Gazette* firmly in 1785,

are looked for with great expectation by the literati of Europe; they are anxious to behold in what manner an historian will appear in a country where the press is really free, and not under the trammels of bigotry or ministerial influence.

American historians were indeed already appearing, and there was considerable agreement among them as to the content, theme, and purpose of their work. Samuel Williams in *The Natural and Civil History of Vermont* (1794) put it this way:

To ascertain what there is . . . peculiar and distinguishing in the state of society in the federal Union, to explain the causes which have led to this state, to mark its effect upon human happiness, and to deduce improvement from the whole, are the most important objects which civil history can contemplate in America: And they are objects, every where more useful to men, than any refinements, distinctions, or discoveries, merely speculative.

David Ramsay was more specific in his *History of South-Carolina* (1809):

Of their [the United States'] wars, and their late revolution much has been written, but a development of the causes which in less than two centuries have raised them from poverty to riches—from ignorance to knowledge—from weakness to power—from a handful of people to a mighty multitude—from rude woodsmen to polished citizens—from colonists guided by the leading strings of a distant island to a well regulated self-governed community, has not been sufficiently the subject of attention.

4

For the Am. Philos. Society,
Philada
from
W. Barton
Aug. 17th. 1792.

THE

HISTORY

OF THE PROVINCE OF

NEW-YORK,

FROM THE FIRST DISCOVERY TO THE YEAR 1732.

To which is annexed, a defcription of the country, with
a fhort account of the inhabitants, their reli-
gious and political ftate, and the con-
ftitution of the courts of juf-
tice in that colony.

Lo! fwarming o'er the new difcover'd world,
Gay colonies extend; the calm retreat
Of undeferv'd diftrefs.——————   THOMSON.

Nec minor eft virtus, quam quærere, parta tueri.

THE SECOND EDITION.

BY WILLIAM SMITH, A.M.

PHILADELPHIA:

FROM THE PRESS OF MATHEW CAREY.

APRIL 9—M.DCC.XCII.

1. William Smith. *The History of the Province of New-York.*
Second edition, Philadelphia, 1792.

In rapid succession in the two decades following the peace
of Paris histories appeared of Maine, Vermont, New Hampshire, Connecticut, Pennsylvania, Virginia, North and South
Carolina; and the Philadelphia publisher Mathew Carey,
"at the desire of several gentlemen of taste," began to repub-
lish some of the earlier colonial histories, like William Smith's
New York (1792). Although not often achieving the high pur-
poses Williams and Ramsay set for them, each of the histories

5

THE

NATURAL AND CIVIL

HISTORY

OF

VERMONT.

BY SAMUEL WILLIAMS, LL. D.

MEMBER OF THE METEOROLOGICAL SOCIETY IN GERMA-
NY, OF THE PHILOSOPHICAL SOCIETY IN PHILADE-
PHIA, AND OF THE ACADEMY OF ARTS AND SCIENCE
IN MASSACHUSETTS.

Published according to ACT *of* CONGRESS.

PRINTED AT *WALPOLE*, NEWHAMPSHIRE,
BY ISAIAH THOMAS AND DAVID CARLISLE, JUN,
Sold at their BOOKSTORE, in *Walpole*, and by said THOMAS, at his
BOOKSTORE, in *Worcester*.
MDCCXCIV.

2. Samuel Williams. *The Natural and Civil History of Vermont*
(Walpole, N.H., 1794).

THE

HISTORY

OF THE *Jn Vaughan*

DISTRICT

OF

MAINE.

By JAMES SULLIVAN.

Illuſtrated by a new correct M A P of the DISTRICT.

Boston.

PRINTED BY I. THOMAS AND E. T. ANDREWS,

FAUST'S STATUE, No. NEWBURY STREET.

1795.

3. James Sullivan. *The History of the District of Maine* (Boston, 1795).

was regarded, as the *Columbian Magazine* said of Ramsay's *History of the Revolution of South-Carolina* (1785), as another step toward the realization of "that independence, which for some years after the termination of the late arduous conflict with Britain, existed only in name."

These narratives, untrammelled by bigotry or ministerial influence, were set against the broad background that independence and the establishment of the federal union offered. Though one or two authors, like Trumbull of Connecticut and John Burk of Virginia, imagined that American history was the history of their own states writ large, most took a middle view, believing with James Sullivan, author of *The History of the District of Maine* (1795), that their books would "aid in the completion of a perfect history of United America." The sentiment was not only modest, but sensible and even necessary, for "a perfect history of United America" could best be written only after the stories of the states were told, providing the national historian with bases for his generalizations. Indeed, many aspects of life had no national history at all, as the authors of the early state histories understood.

These historians took a broad view of the history and life of the people they described. A quotation on the title page of Ramsay's *History of South-Carolina* perfectly expressed their idea: "The Muse of history has been so much in love with Mars, that she has seldom conversed with Minerva." The histories accordingly often contained natural history as well as civil. Only a quarter of Williams' *History of Vermont* was given over to political narrative; the remainder dealt with geography, the Indian inhabitants, natural history, employments, religion, laws, population, customs, freedom, and "the State of Society." Every historian presented data and records of birth rates, life expectancy, and longevity—all matters of interest and concern in an underpopulated country. The in-

8

clusion of such data was not an expression of the prejudices of idiosyncratic authors; the questions which historians asked were not unimportant if the entire range of the people's lives was to be displayed—and historical societies addressed them as well as individual authors. The earliest volumes of the *Collections* of the Massachusetts Historical Society, for example, printed articles on earthquakes, meteors, ocean and dust storms, instructions for preserving the skins of birds and animals, and—in Volume 5 (1798)—Professor William Dandridge Peck's essay on the "Natural History of the Slug-Worm."

The state historians sought authoritative sources wherever they might be found, but the search was not easy. Not a few, on finishing their books, warmly declared that, had they known what the search entailed, they would never have begun. That was not a conventional disclaimer. There were no central depositories of records then, hardly a depository anywhere except the desks of town clerks and church ministers. At great expense of time and effort the historian had to travel through the countryside, looking up oldest inhabitants, copying books and manuscripts in the "garrets and ratholes of old houses" (as Benjamin Trumbull did in Prince's library), even tramping through cemeteries to glean an elusive name or date from weatherworn gravestones. David Ramsay circulated a questionnaire asking for data on settlements, Indian inhabitants, topography, soils, the state of cultivation, appropriate sites for mills and factories, and "singular instances of longevity and fecundity." Hugh Williamson went farther afield: through friends travelling in England he obtained (despite obstructions thrown up by George Chalmers) copies of documents on North Carolina in the British Museum and public records offices; and a gentleman in Berne procured for him copies of the correspondence of Baron de Graffenreid. Older authors had to be read and appraised: Burk thought

Beverley "a mere annalist of petty incidents," and dismissed Captain John Smith's *General Historie of Virginia* as "a sort of epic history or romance." And then, when the narrative was composed at last, the newly-discovered facts and revised judgments might be spread out in an appendix of "Proofs and Explanations." Jeremy Belknap, historian of New Hampshire (1784), concluded from his own experience that "there are required so many qualifications and accomplishments in an Historian, and so much care and niceness in writing an history that some have reckoned it one of the most difficult labors human nature is capable of."

Then as now an especially popular kind of historical writing was biographical. To know who had discovered and explored the country, established and governed the settlements was almost a prerequisite for narration—the taxonomy of history. Belknap began in the 1780s to collect biographical notes for an "American Plutarch" (the title the editors of the *Dictionary of American Biography* gave to a recently published volume of selections from that work); and the first sketches— of Governor John Winthrop, Sir Fernando Gorges, and Captain John Smith—were printed in the *Columbian Magazine* in 1788. Belknap eventually completed his *American Biography* in two volumes (1794–98); the sketches, beginning with Bjorn and Madoc, were arranged chronologically to tell the history of America. In 1809 two collections of biographies were published. One was John Eliot's *Biographical Dictionary . . . of . . . New England*, characterized by a Yankee crankiness and regret for a vanished happy age when, as he believed, "there was order in the cities, peace in the villages, and religion in the Temples." The other was *An American Biographical and Historical Dictionary* by William Allen, assistant librarian of Harvard College. Unlike Eliot's dictionary, which was limited to New England, Allen's was national in scope, containing 700 sketches, based on a wide variety of sources, and might

AMERICAN BIOGRAPHY:

O R,

An HISTORICAL ACCOUNT

Of those PERSONS

WHO HAVE BEEN DISTINGUISHED IN

A M E R I C A,

A S

ADVENTURERS,	DIVINES,
STATESMEN,	WARRIORS,
PHILOSOPHERS,	AUTHORS,

And other REMARKABLE CHARACTERS.

Comprehending a Recital of

The EVENTS connected with their LIVES and ACTIONS.

V O L. I.

By JEREMY BELKNAP, D. D.

" Hic manus ob patriam pugnando vulnera paffi :
Quique facerdotes cafti, cum vita manebat :
Quique pii vates, et Phœbo digna locuti :
Inventas aut qui vitam excoluere per artes :
Quique fui memores alios fecere merendo :"
VIRGIL, Æn. vj. 660.

Published according to Act of Congrefs.

PRINTED at *BOSTON*,
By ISAIAH THOMAS and EBENEZER T. ANDREWS.
Faust's Statue, No 45, Newbury Street.
MDCCXCIV.

4. Jeremy Belknap. *American Biography* (Boston, 1794).

have contained 200 more. The work was expanded twice, the third edition with 7000 entries appearing in 1857.

Other biographical dictionaries followed—of lawyers and judges by Samuel A. Knapp (1821), signers of the Declaration of Independence by John Sanderson (1820), and physicians by James Thacher (1828). These biographers believed they illustrated American history through lives. "My object," Knapp declared, "has been to give in connection with these notices of individuals, something of the history of the manners, habits and institutions of New England." More than this, the biographical dictionaries included not only the great and famous but "many others less imposing . . . nearer the level of human nature," of whom what was related "has a more common application and use." Allen believed his dictionary had a more intimate use—wherever possible he included a description of the last hours of his subject that readers might be instructed by the record of this awful moment "beyond which the next step will either plunge him . . . into an abyss, from which he will never rise, or will elevate him to everlasting glory. . . ."

And always they worked with a sense of urgency. Each year precious documents were lost or destroyed or, if preserved in private hands, became more difficult to trace, not always accessible if found. Impressed with these thoughts, wishing to preserve documents and make them available "by multiplying copies," Ebenezer Hazard undertook his life work. A graduate of the College of New Jersey, he was a printer and bookseller in New York in 1774, when, on the eve of the assembling of the First Continental Congress, he proposed in a circular letter that a collection of American public documents be made and published.

When the Conduct of Individuals in a Community is such as to attract public Attention, others are very naturally led to many Inquiries about them; so when civil States rise into Importance, even their earliest History becomes the object of Speculation. From a Principle of Curiosity, many who have but little, or no Connection with the British Colonies in America, are now prying into the Story of their rise and progress, while others wish for a farther Acquaintance with them, from better, though perhaps more interested Motives. The Means of obtaining this Information are not accessible by every Person and if they were, are so scattered, that more Time would be necessary for collecting them, than would be requisite for reading them after they were collected.

To remove this Obstruction from the path of Science, and at the same Time to lay the Foundation of a good American History, by preserving from oblivion valuable Materials for the Purpose, . . .

Despite war and wartime preoccupations, Hazard kept his project alive. The prospect of independence in fact strengthened his conviction that the authentic sources for American history should be collected and published. "Gratitude to heaven and to our virtuous fathers, justice to ourselves, and a becoming regard to posterity," he wrote, "strongly urge us to an improvement of it before time and accident deprive us of the means." Accordingly in 1778 he petitioned Congress for countenance and support. Congress recommended Hazard's undertaking to the several states, gave him access to its papers, and authorized $1,000 for his expenses (though it does not appear the money was ever appropriated). As postmaster general, however, Hazard enjoyed some advantages: he could combine archival searches with post office business in distant places and, thanks to the franking privilege, could correspond on historical subjects at practically no cost. Work proceeded slowly, and Hazard sometimes despaired of publication. He once considered disposing of the collection to the Library Company of Philadelphia, and even thought of selling the copyright to a British publisher, but that idea implied "something so disreputable to the Union," that he rejected it. The first volume appeared at last in 1792, a second in 1794; but the remaining projected volumes, which would have contained documents from other colonies than New England, were never issued.

What Hazard could not do alone, historical societies, libraries, and other learned associations of individuals might do with some prospect of success. The Massachusetts Historical Society was founded in 1791 to collect, preserve, and publish materials of history. Another historical society was established in New York in 1804. Farther south, in Philadelphia, long the political and at this time still the cultural capital of the nation, historical collecting took another form. The successes and failures—and the reasons for them—of the Historical and Literary Committee of the American Philosophical Society are themselves an instructive tale.

At a regular meeting of the Society on June 21, 1811, Peter S. Du Ponceau, a lawyer with an extensive knowledge of languages and a sympathetic interest in American history, called for a committee to collect materials for, and make researches in, the history of the United States in general and of Pennsylvania in particular. The resolution was referred to the officers of the Society. Perhaps predictably, they opposed it. Some members pointed out that history was nowhere mentioned in the Society's charter as an object of its concern; others feared that cultivation of history would divert the philosophers from their true purpose—knowledge of the first settlements, they seemed to say, was less useful than knowledge of the breeding habits of the Hessian fly. Du Ponceau replied that failure to mention history should not be construed to forbid attention to it; and furthermore that cultivation of knowledge and understanding of the past could in fact be fairly claimed as "promoting useful knowledge," which was the Society's announced purpose. But there was no consensus, and no action was taken. Nonetheless, Du Ponceau's motion had excited historical interest among the members of the Society;

so that when it was reported in 1812 that one Joseph Anthony, a goldsmith in High Street, possessed a curious ancient parchment, the Society despatched a committee forthwith to ask him for it—and that is why visitors to Philosophical Hall today may see the original Charter of Privileges which William Penn granted to the inhabitants of Pennsylvania in 1701.

Du Ponceau renewed his proposal in 1815. This time it met with a warmer reception. The reason, Du Ponceau later explained, was the new spirit in the nation.

In the year 1815, was received the joyful news of the peace with Great Britain. Until that period, a colonial spirit has prevailed throughout the country, that had checked all efforts at literary enterprize. The successful issue of the war raised our spirits; and our minds took a direction towards literature and science.

This new committee—the seventh of the Society's standing committees—was empowered to collect "Original Documents, such as Official and Private Letters, Indian Treaties, Ancient Records, Ancient Maps, and such other Papers as may be calculated to throw light on the History of the United States, but more particularly this State," and to correspond with eligible persons throughout the country on history, geography, topography, antiquities, and statistics of the country. Everything of this nature collected was to be preserved "for the public benefit." From all this activity it was confidently expected that

Zeal will be reciprocally excited, emulation kept up, & the future historians of our Country will bless the patriotic hands that are now providing for them the ample Stores out of which . . . American Livies & Tacituses will compose immortal histories for the benefit of posterity.

The Committee lost no time in organizing. William Tilghman, chief justice of the Commonwealth, was chosen chairman; John Vaughan, librarian of the Society, was recording secretary; and Du Ponceau took the strategic post of corresponding secretary. Another active member until his death in 1818 was Dr. Caspar Wistar, professor of anatomy in the Medical School of the University of Pennsylvania and Thomas Jefferson's successor as president of the Philosophical Society. These four made an interesting group, not least because three of them were not natives of Pennsylvania, two not even native Americans.

Judge Tilghman, born in Maryland, was educated at the College of Philadelphia. Son of an officer of the Pennsylvania proprietary government, Tilghman was a Loyalist during the Revolution, his brother Philemon served in the British Navy, and his brother Tench was one of Washington's aides—dramatic evidence that the American war with Britain was also a civil war and an intriguing suggestion that an aristocratic society seems better able than a democratic one to judge a man on his own character. After the war Tilghman served in the Maryland Assembly, then in 1793 moved to the capital, where he had a distinguished career at the bar and in the federal judiciary, and was named chief justice of Pennsylvania in 1806. John Vaughan was an English Whig, who came to America after the Revolution with his father and brothers, settled as a merchant in Philadelphia, and for 50 years until his death in 1841 served the Philosophical Society as treasurer and librarian, tirelessly collecting books and manuscripts, compiling the library's first printed catalogue, an affable host at breakfasts to which he invited distinguished strangers in town, and becoming at last himself one of the monuments and memorable sights of the city. Wistar was a conscientious philanthropic Quaker, president of the Abolition Society, a friend to the Indians and one of the first to comment on their eloquence in council. For many years it was his custom to invite friends to his home on Saturdays for

5. John Vaughan (1756–1841). By Thomas Sully.

an evening of good talk; when he died they unanimously re-
solved that so agreeable a practice should not be abandoned
and so organized The Wistar Association, which, 160 years
later, meets regularly in the very pattern he established. To
one of the first meetings of the Historical Committee Wistar
brought a list of historical topics to be inquired into, with
suggestions where books and documents with desired information might be found. As he had so obviously thought

6. Peter Stephen Du Ponceau (1760–1844). By Thomas Sully.

about a program, Wistar's fellow-members on the Committee promptly appointed him to develop a practicable plan for a biographical dictionary.

But the most unusual and tireless member of the Committee was Du Ponceau himself. A French Protestant who had come to America in 1777 as military secretary and interpreter to Baron von Steuben, Du Ponceau studied law after the war, specializing in civil law and serving particularly those who had business in France, Holland, Germany, and Russia. Despite nearsightedness that is painfully or comically apparent in every portrait and caricature, Du Ponceau was a tireless student and writer. He was to be president of the American Philosophical Society, the Historical Society of Pennsylvania, the Athenaeum of Philadelphia, and the Pennsylvania Library of Foreign Literature—simultaneously.

As corresponding secretary of the Historical and Literary Committee Du Ponceau addressed his first letter to Thomas Jefferson, partly as a courtesy to the president of the Philosophical Society, but primarily because Jefferson was, in Du Ponceau's words, "a friend to American Science & Literature." Jefferson responded warmly: the Society, he thought, had been "too much confined *in practice* to the Natural and Mathematical departments"; and he sent along a manuscript description of the country of the Creek Indians written by Colonel Benjamin Hawkins, an agent among them. Such loose sheets, Jefferson continued, "of no use by themselves and in the hands of the holders," became "of great value when brought together into a general depot, open to the use of the future historian or literary enquirer." Other gifts from Monticello followed; and Du Ponceau enlisted Jefferson's help in identifying and augmenting the imperfect copy of William Byrd's History of the Dividing Line, which the Society had recently been given. Files of newspapers, Du Ponceau explained to Alexander Graydon of Harrisburg, were especially valuable because, "more than any thing else [they gave] the true form and pressure of the times in which they were published." Historical and statistical notes on the several counties and boroughs of the state were solicited—though the response was far less than in Massachusetts, where scholarly ministers of an established church so often took the lead in answering inquiries. At the same time, in their regular meetings the Committee members were full of questions:

Dear Sir   Monticello Jan. 22. 16.

    I have been 4. of the last 5. months absent from home, which must apologise for this very tardy acknolegement of your favor of Nov. 14. I learn with much satisfaction the enlargement by the Philosophical society of the scope of their institution, by the establishment of a standing committee for history, the moral sciences and general literature. I have always thought that we were too much confined in practice to the Natural and Mathematical departments. this Committee will become a depository for many original MS. many loose sheets, of no use by themselves and in the hands of the holder, but of great value when brought into a general depot, open to the use of the future historian or literary enquirer.   I shall be very happy in contributing to the usefulness of your establishment by any thing in my possession, or within the reach of my endeavors; and I begin by inclosing you a geographical and statistical account in MS. of the Creek or Muscogee Indians and country, as it was in the years 98. and 99. this was written by Colo. Hawkins who has lived among them as agent now upwards of 20. years. besides a general interspersion of observations on the state of society, manners and opinions among them, there is in the latter part an interesting account of their government, & ceremonies, civil and religious; the more valuable as we have so little information of the civil regimen of the Indian nations.   I think it probable I may find other things on my shelves, or among my papers, worth preserving with you, and will with pleasure forward them from time to time, as I lay my hands on them.

    Of the MS. journal of the Commissioners of 1728. on the North Carolina boundary, I cannot give you positive information. it has always been understood that the Westover family possessed

    M. Du Ponceau

7. Thomas Jefferson. Letter to Peter S. Du Ponceau, January 22, 1816, congratulating the American Philosophical Society on adding history to its fields of interest.

MEMOIRS

OF A LIFE,

CHIEFLY PASSED IN PENNSYLVANIA,
WITHIN THE LAST SIXTY YEARS;

WITH OCCASIONAL REMARKS
UPON THE GENERAL OCCURRENCES,
CHARACTER AND SPIRIT
OF THAT EVENTFUL PERIOD.

》-※-*《*

HARRISBURGH:
PRINTED BY JOHN WYETH.
1 8 1 1.

8. Alexander Graydon. *Memoirs of a Life, Chiefly Passed in Pennsylvania . . .* (Harrisburg, Pa., 1811).

where could they obtain facts about the March of the Paxton Boys 50 years before? Who could write a biography of the historian Robert Proud? A life of James Logan was wanted as well; and so were sketches of Benjamin Smith Barton, Jonathan Williams, Benjamin Rush, Alexander J. Dallas, James Wilson, and Dupont de Nemours, all of whom were but recently dead. The Philadelphians, Du Ponceau would explain, aimed at making "a Complete historical library relative to the State of Pennsylvania, at least, if not all the United

States. . . ." Americans must preserve and write their own history, else they would suffer the unhappy fate of the Carthaginians, whose history was known only from the pens of their enemies.

In general the response was encouraging. Most of Du Ponceau's correspondents promised to search for old papers in their possession or to organize their recollections on particular points. The Reverend Mr. Henry Augustus Muhlenberg of Reading, for example, promised an account of Conrad Weiser's coming from Schoharie to Tulpehocken, and Senator Andrew Gregg of Bellefonte promised to write a sketch of General James Potter of the Pennsylvania Line in the Revolution. From Dr. George Logan of Stenton, his brother-in-law Joseph Parker Norris, and from William Rawle came precious documents, printed proclamations and handbills of William Penn's time. When Du Ponceau discovered that one of these had been printed in Clarkson's life of Penn, he was excited and puzzled how that could be—the letter apparently had been locked up in the Rawle family papers "from time immemorial."

As was to be expected, of course, some inquiries brought no replies, and other answers were disappointing. General Joseph Bloomfield of New Jersey told the Committee that he had promised East Jersey documents in his possession to the New-York Historical Society; and John Lardner, son of a proprietary official, reported that he had turned over to the Commonwealth all documents of a public nature and that, "desirous that myself & family should live in peace with all men," he had destroyed his father's personal correspondence. (In fact, Lardner could not bring himself to commit so drastic an act of destruction; the papers survived; and a century and a half later were presented by a descendant to the Historical Society of Pennsylvania.) One night it was reported that Benjamin Waller of Williamsburg, Va., had found "some ancient letters in a Trunk, some of which related to public affairs 100 Years back," and on another a descendant of General Joseph Reed produced "Two Bundles of Letters" written by Washington to the Continental Congress; but neither the Waller nor the Reed letters came to the Historical Committee. One elderly Quaker, famous for other-mindedness, inquired what he should do with papers he owned on the early years of the province. "Give them to the Philosophical Society," he was advised. He considered this a few moments, then replied, "I believe I had best keep them myself."

Though the membership of the Historical and Literary Committee was never large, and attendance at its meetings was necessarily small, discussions were often lively and usually instructive. Judge Tilghman remembered how, when the business of the evening was concluded, the members would draw their chairs around the fire, exchanging historical anecdotes and speculations as the hours wore on to midnight. One evening someone reported that Miers Fisher, the Quaker lawyer, had said that he had heard Richard Bache declare in open court that he had heard his father-in-law Benjamin Franklin assert unequivocally that he was not the author of the *Historical Review of Pennsylvania*; to which someone else rejoined that Mrs. Deborah Logan, a reservoir of historical fact and lore, declared positively that Franklin was indeed the author. Joseph Sansom, traveller, artist, and connoisseur, offered strictures on the accuracy of John Trumbull's painting of the Signing of the Declaration of Independence. Another told how Tedyusking, chief of the Delawares, satisfied with the accuracy of Charles Thomson's minutes of an Indian conference, took the white man by the hand and to all present announced, "He is *my secretary*; he is correct." Correa da Serra, voicing his alarm that physical traces of olden times were rapidly disappearing, proposed in 1819 that the Committee take a plan of the lines and redoubts the British con-

A

PETITION

PRESENTED BY

Capt. *Alexander Patterson,*

TO THE

LEGISLATURE OF PENNSYLVANIA,

DURING

The Seffion of 1803—4, for Compenfation for the *Monies*
he *Expended* and the *Services* he *Rendered* in *Defence*

OF THE

PENNSYLVANIA TITLE,

AGAINST THE

CONNECTICUT CLAIMANTS;

IN WHICH IS COMPRISED,

A faithful hiftorical detail of *important* and *interefting* FACTS
and EVENTS that took place at *Wyoming,* and
in the county of *Luzerne, &c.*

IN CONSEQUENCE

OF THE

DISPUTE WHICH EXISTED

BETWEEN THE

PENNSYLVANIA LAND-HOLDERS,

AND THE

CONNECTICUT INTRUDERS,

Commencing with the Year, 1763.

LANCASTER:
PRINTED BY ROBERT BAILEY, SOUTH
QUEEN-STREET.
1804.

9. *A Petition presented by Capt. Alexander Patterson, to the Legislature of Pennsylvania. . . .* (Lancaster, 1804). One of the "Wyoming pamphlets" promised to the Historical and Literary Committee by Dr. Thomas Cooper but actually presented by Judge John Bannister Gibson.

structed around the city in 1777 and 1778 before they were totally obliterated.

The more books and documents came in, of course, the more eager the Committee was for more; and the members had suggestions where desirable items might be found. Dr. Thomas Cooper, who had just come to Philadelphia from four turbulent years in Carlisle as professor of chemistry in Dickinson College, thought he could get copies of almost all the pamphlets printed on the Wyoming controversy; as it turned out it was Judge John Bannister Gibson, another Carlisle resident, who presented two bundles of pamphlets on the subject. Charles Smith of Lancaster was urged to search his attic for the correspondence and other papers of his father, the politically active Provost William Smith of the College of Philadelphia. Dr. Wistar, returning from a trip through Bucks and Berks Counties, informed his colleagues of the whereabouts of a manuscript account of the settlement at Buckingham, a journal of Conrad Weiser, and documents on the settlement of the Juniata and upper Susquehanna Valleys. The papers of General Anthony Wayne, the Committee was informed, were in possession of his son in Chester County, and those of General Edward Hand in that of Samuel Bechtel of Columbia. (Both collections eventually came to the Historical Society of Pennsylvania.) William Rawle asked John Penn in England, the Founder's grandson, for a selection of "important documents relative to the early Settlements." (The Penn Papers, too, eventually went to the Historical Society.) Dr. George Logan gave the Committee William Penn's cash book, rough minutes of the Proprietary Council, and selections from the correspondence of his grandfather James Logan, Penn's secretary and the Province's chief justice.

When original documents could not be acquired, the Committee made efforts to assemble copies of official records. Correa da Serra, for example, suggested that Pennsylvania

10. John Gottlieb Ernestus Heckewelder (1743–1823). By John Lewis Krimmel.

records in the Colonial Office in London be copied; and the Committee duly inquired of the American Minister how this could be done. Redmond Conyngham, secretary of the Commonwealth, procured copies of scores of provincial records at Harrisburg. And Jonathan Russell of Massachusetts, formerly the American minister at Stockholm, sent along copies

11. John Heckewelder. Letter to Peter S. Du Ponceau, May 27, 1816, answering the latter's queries about the Delaware Indians.

of documents of American interest which he had had made in the Swedish archives, including a copy and translation of Acrelius' *History of New Sweden*.

Of all Du Ponceau's correspondents, however, none was so

faithful or so prolific as John Heckewelder, Moravian missionary to the Indians, now living in retirement at Bethlehem; and with none did Du Ponceau so rejoice in exchanging information and opinions on the languages, customs, and history of the Indians. Wistar had told each man about the other, and long before they met Du Ponceau was soliciting

occasional Communications on the various Subjects that are familiar to you & which relate to the early history of this Country. Accounts of the various Nations of Indians which have at different times inhabited Pennsylvania, their Number, Origin, migrations, connexions with each other, the parts which they took in the English & French Wars & in the Revolutionary War, their manners, customs, languages, religion, in Short, every thing which you may conceive interesting on a Subject, which at no distant period will be involved in obscurity & doubt, for want of the proper Information having been given in time by those Contemporaries who now possess the requisite knowledge and are still able to communicate it.

Queries streamed out of Philadelphia: what was the etymology of calumet, tomahawk, wampum, papoose, sagamore, savannah, and other Indian words commonly used by the English? Do the Indians learn English easily? How can one reconcile the Delawares' tradition that they came from across the Mississippi with the fact that their language is of the same stock as that of eastern Indians? "I confess that my knowledge is very limited," Du Ponceau wrote in explanation and apology. "I Seek the Truth, & Seek it humbly & honestly." Both men appreciated the language of the Indians. "You speak to a convert when you observe upon the richness of the American languages," Du Ponceau told Heckewelder.

I am struck, particularly, with their Grammatical forms, by means of which they combine with admirable regularity & order a great number of ideas in one single word. For Example: *Wulomalessohalion! O thou who makest me happy!* There is no language in

TRANSACTIONS

OF THE

HISTORICAL & LITERARY COMMITTEE

OF THE

AMERICAN PHILOSOPHICAL SOCIETY,

HELD AT PHILADELPHIA, FOR PROMOTING

USEFUL KNOWLEDGE.

—

VOL. I.

Invenies illic et facta domestica vobis ;
Sæpè tibi pater est, sæpè legendus avus.—OVID.

PHILADELPHIA:

Printed and Published by Abraham Small,

No. 112, Chesnut Street,

1819.

12. Historical and Literary Committee of the American Philosophical Society. *Transactions*, I (Philadelphia, 1819).

the old world, ancient or modern, that I have ever heard or known of, that offers such a beautiful word, regularly derived, conjugated, & declined. . . .

Back and forth flew comments and criticisms of the writings of James Adair, Father Charlevoix, Roger Williams, Jonathan Edwards, Jonathan Carver, Loskiel, Lahontan, Vater, and John Eliot, for a new edition of whose Indian grammar, edited by John Pickering and published by the Massachusetts Historical Society in 1822, Du Ponceau prepared 56 pages of Notes and Observations. Many of these letters, together with a dictionary of the Onondaga language, a list of Delaware words, and a history of the Indians of Pennsylvania, which Heckewelder sent to Philadelphia, were published in the first volume of the *Transactions* of the Historical and Literary Committee (1819). It was Isaiah Thomas' judgment that "certainly nothing any way equal to it for an account of the aboriginals of this country, was ever before published." Additional testimony to its usefulness came in a request for copies for the instruction of young missionaries in the West.

Despite the interest it generated and the unquestionably valuable acquisitions it made for the Society's library, the Historical and Literary Committee cannot be said to have been successful. Certainly the expectation that a good history of Pennsylvania would be written from its labors remained unfulfilled, as Du Ponceau admitted in an address to the Society in 1821.

It was hoped that the impulse thus given would have been caught by some able writer, who, availing himself of these rich stores, would have combined the scattered facts into a faithful and elegant narrative. But our expectations have hitherto been deceived, and Pennsylvania still wants an historian.

In that respect, and to that extent, the Philadelphians had done less than they hoped toward creating a national spirit.

Worcester, Mass. Sept. 20th 1819.

John Vaughan, Esqr. Secy.
of the Historical Comee. of
the American Philosophical
Society, Philadelphia.

Isaiah Thomas

rec'd First Vol

Sir,

I was, sometime since, honoured by the reception
of your letter of the 21st of February last, together with
that truly valuable work, "Transactions of the Historical and
Literary Committee of the American Philosophical Society,
Vol. I." presented to me by said Committee, and conveyed to me
by the politeness of the Rev. President of Harvard University,
as was, also, a copy of the same work for the American Anti-
quarian Society.

The government of the society last mentioned, have
directed their Secretary to transmit (through Mr. Walsh, your
corresponding Secretary) their thanks for this valuable
donation; and I requested the Secretary of this society, in his
letter, to make my acknowledgment to the Historical and Literary
Committee for the copy presented to me, and to mention a few
observations which occurred to me on perusing the book. It
is unnecessary to repeat to you these observations, but I cannot
forbear to remark that I have been highly gratified in reading
this volume; certainly nothing any way equal to it, for an
account of the aborigines of this country, was ever before
published. The public are under great obligation to the
venerable Mr. Heckewelder for his communications, and to Dr.
Du Ponceau for his researches and indefatigable labours in bringing
forward a work so greatly interesting to the Literati of both
hemispheres.

I beg

13. Isaiah Thomas. Letter to John Vaughan, September 20,
1819, acknowledging receipt of the *Transactions* of the Historical
and Literary Committee of the American Philosophical Society.

There were important reasons for this failure. The Committee's members were drawn from the rolls of the parent Society, to which most persons were elected for other reasons than interest in historical research. Thus the Historical Committee would always be small and could never include the many historically-minded Philadelphians who, though not members of the Philosophical Society, would gladly have joined in an historical association. Furthermore, those who did join the Society's seventh committee at best gave its work only intermittent attention. "We are going on in this Country with researches on the Indians & their languages," Du Ponceau assured Johann Vater in 1821; then lamented, "but unfortunately we are all professional men, who have our business to attend to"—(but this excuse is the same almost any American might have offered at the time for not promoting some cultural institution). In short, the Committee received scant moral, and no financial, support from the Society as a whole; it received none from the larger community; and attempts to get assistance from the Commonwealth were halfhearted and predictably fruitless.

No less important than this constitutional defect as a reason for failure was the domination of the Committee by Peter Du Ponceau. Though genuinely interested in history and the author of several papers of merit, his consuming passion was languages and linguistics. It was appropriate that the Committee should be interested in the Indians; but Du Ponceau narrowed that concern to the study of their languages, and then made that study the almost exclusive concern of the Committee. The first volume of its *Transactions*, for example, was filled entirely with such materials; the second contained a long dissertation by Du Ponceau on the Chinese system of writing and a Cochinchinese vocabulary compiled by Father Joseph Morrone. Few persons, in or out of the Historical Committee, could be expected to have any interest in these

32

subjects. (In fact, the Society still has a large number of unsold copies, perhaps a third of the edition, of the Cochinchinese dictionary.) Members of the Society and even of the Committee who were interested in history rather than in Indian languages no longer found meetings stimulating or even congenial. The tiny membership dwindled, and no new recruits were received. One member, Roberts Vaux, advised John Fanning Watson not to give the manuscript of his Annals of Philadelphia to the Committee, as Watson first intended.

Just at this period, when it must have seemed that history was everywhere neglected in Philadelphia (the Commonwealth of Pennsylvania only a few years before had offered the old State House for sale at $70,000—bell and all; the city purchased the building for reasons of utility) two events occurred that stimulated historical enterprise. The first was the visit to General Lafayette to Philadelphia in the fall of 1824 on his triumphal return to America as "the Nation's Guest." This happy occasion, which evoked memories of the Revolution, produced a determination to preserve the fast-fading records of that event. The second event, which occurred a few weeks later, was the commemoration of the arrival of William Penn in Pennsylvania in 1682. At that meeting Du Ponceau, who was the speaker of the day, called for an annual commemoration; and the company concluded the exercises by organizing a society for the purpose. Not a few of those who hailed Lafayette and toasted the memory of Penn now determined to establish a historical society, of wide scope, open to all. They were joined, if not led, by Chief Justice Tilghman and other members of the now-moribund Historical and Literary Committee; and early in 1825 the Historical Society of Pennsylvania came into being.

Though the Historical Society was clearly its intellectual offspring, the Philosophical Society at first regarded it as a

33

rival. Ill feeling, perhaps natural in the case, was aggravated when, as one of its first acts, the new society asked to publish Penn and Logan documents that the Historical Committee had collected; and the latter refused to hand them over. Tension soon relaxed, however; and Rawle and Du Ponceau, both active members of the Historical and Literary Committee, became in succession presidents of the Historical Society. Though it began bravely enough, held meetings regularly, collected papers and artifacts, and published several volumes of *Memoirs*, the Historical Society apparently soon became inactive. At least an anonymous writer in the *National Gazette* of July 20, 1841, condemned the "sluggishness" in local historical activity.

We have a Historical Society that does little, a Historical Committee of the Philosophical Society, which does less, and a William Penn Society, or something of the sort that does nothing. Thus with the necessary material for vigorously carrying on the siege, all hands lie down in the trenches and go to sleep! This state of things is discreditable to Philadelphia.

Though perhaps too sweeping, the stricture certainly applied to the Historical and Literary Committee of the Philosophical Society. After the founding of the Historical Society, the Committee effectively ceased to exist. John Heckewelder died in 1823; for a few years Du Ponceau maintained a desultory correspondence with others on Indian languages; then in 1834 he handed over to John Vaughan all the Committee's records and correspondence. There was a fitful revival in 1843. Historical papers read at the Society's centennial celebration that year—one by Samuel Breck on Continental currency, accompanied by scores of specimens—were deemed unsuitable for the scientific *Proceedings*, and so they were published as Part I of Volume 3 of the *Transactions* of the Historical and Literary Committee. There was never a Part II.

Sep. 18. 1840 – Rec.

Chesnut Post Sep. 17/40 [#]

Jno Vaughan Esqr

Dear Sir

Upon Conversing with
my Sister respecting the Papers
of Dr. Franklin bequeathed by
[#] Wm. T Franklin Esqr to my Father
we have Concluded they cannot be
better disposed of than by Presenting to the Society of which he was
the founder.

I remain
very Respectfully
Yrs

[#] Grandson of D. B. Franklin   Chas. P. Fox
to whom the Doc.t bequeathed
his Library & MSS   Jno Vaughan Libn of APS

14. Charles P. Fox. Letter to John Vaughan, September 17, 1840,
donating manuscripts of Benjamin Franklin to the American
Philosophical Society.

Historical Sketch of the continental bills of Credit, from the year 1775 to 1781, with specimens thereof.

By Samuel Breck, of Philadelphia. written for the American Philosophical society in 1840.

In presenting to the Philosophical society, specimens of the bills of credit, issued by the Congress of the Colonies, and of the thirteen United States of America, in the years 1775 to 17$\frac{79}{81}$, both inclusive, I may state that, I am old enough to have seen them in circulation, as the principal currency of the Country; intermixed, however, with Emissions from most of the Colonies, in their

15. Samuel Breck. "Historical Sketch of the Continental Bills of Credit . . . with specimens thereof," 1840. The manuscript was later published.

History of the United States and of Pennsylvania was not again to be a major interest of the Philosophical Society. But, one may believe, neither history nor science suffered by the decision. Just as the founding of the Boston Natural History Society relieved the Massachusetts Historical Society from any lingering responsibility to account for the slug worms of New England, so the founding of the Historical Society in Philadelphia allowed the Philosophical Society to turn its full attention to the Hessian fly, mastodons, and meteor showers. What Du Ponceau's committee had collected, however, remained in the Society's hall and possession; and from time to time other materials came in, like the bulk of Franklin's papers, whose owner had been encouraged by Jared Sparks to donate them to the Society. There in Philosophical Hall in the State House Yard the collections were preserved, not often used, but rediscovered by Paul Leicester Ford and others at the end of the century, when historians of America began to use them systematically (as they continue to do)—a small but valuable part of those ample stores of books and manuscripts, collected also in Charleston, Richmond, New York, Worcester, Boston, and other places, from which—to quote Du Ponceau—American Livies and Tacituses have composed instructive histories that have benefited posterity, not least by helping to shape a national spirit.

One thousand copies
designed and set in type by The Stinehour Press
and printed by The Meriden Gravure Company
on 80-pound S-N Text
Five hundred additional copies for the
Friends of the American Philosophical Society Library